STANDARD GRADE | GENERAL

FRENCH
2008-2012

2008 EXAM — page 3
2008 General Level Reading – 2008 General Level Listening Transcript – 2008 General Level Listening

2009 EXAM — page 25
2009 General Level Reading – 2009 General Level Listening Transcript – 2009 General Level Listening

2010 EXAM — page 45
2010 General Level Reading – 2010 General Level Listening Transcript – 2010 General Level Listening

2011 EXAM — page 67
2011 General Level Reading – 2011 General Level Listening Transcript – 2011 General Level Listening

2012 EXAM — page 89
2012 General Level Reading – 2012 General Level Listening Transcript – 2012 General Level Listening

ANSWER SECTION — page 113

© Scottish Qualifications Authority
All rights reserved. Copying prohibited. No part of this publication may be reproduced, stored in a retrieval system, or transmitted in any form or by any means, electronic, mechanical, photocopying, recording or otherwise.

First exam published in 2008.
Published by Bright Red Publishing Ltd, 6 Stafford Street, Edinburgh EH3 7AU
tel: 0131 220 5804 fax: 0131 220 6710 info@brightredpublishing.co.uk www.brightredpublishing.co.uk

ISBN 978-1-84948-245-5

A CIP Catalogue record for this book is available from the British Library.

Bright Red Publishing is grateful to the copyright holders, as credited on the final page of the Question Section, for permission to use their material. Every effort has been made to trace the copyright holders and to obtain their permission for the use of copyright material. Bright Red Publishing will be happy to receive information allowing us to rectify any error or omission in future editions.

STANDARD GRADE | GENERAL

2008

OFFICIAL SQA PAST PAPERS   5   GENERAL FRENCH 2008

FOR OFFICIAL USE

G

Total

1000/402

NATIONAL
QUALIFICATIONS
2008

TUESDAY, 13 MAY
10.05 AM – 10.50 AM

**FRENCH
STANDARD GRADE**
General Level
Reading

Fill in these boxes and read what is printed below.

Full name of centre

Town

Forename(s)

Surname

Date of birth
Day Month Year   Scottish candidate number   Number of seat

When you are told to do so, open your paper and write your answers **in English** in the spaces provided.

You may use a French dictionary.

Before leaving the examination room you must give this book to the invigilator. If you do not, you may lose all the marks for this paper.

PB 1000/402 6/36070

1. You are reading a French magazine. This advert about a chain of restaurants attracts your attention.

RESTAURANTS «BONNE BOUFFE»

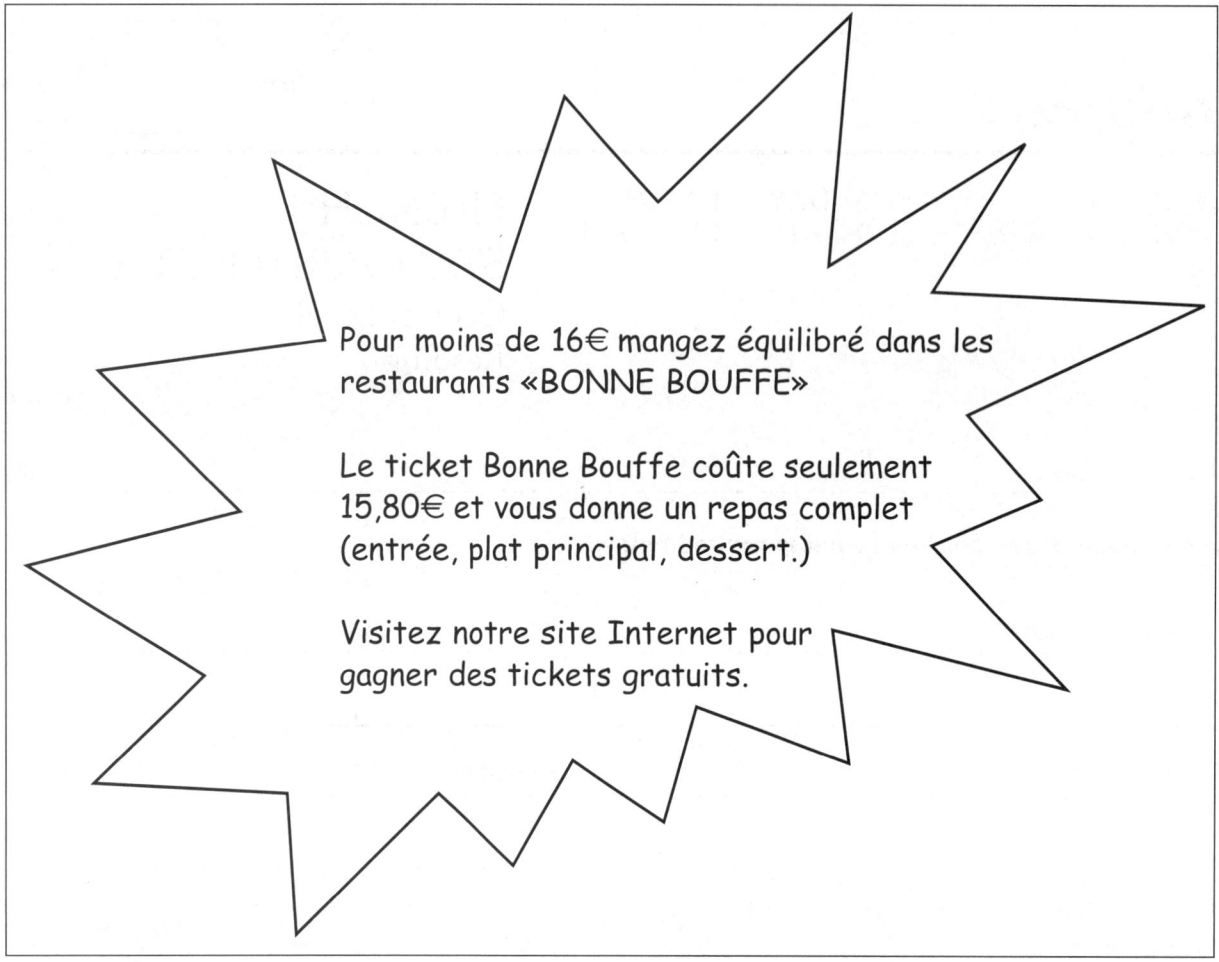

(a) What do you get for a 15,80€ ticket in these restaurants?

(b) Why might you visit their website?

2. You read about a survey on the eating habits of some people in France.

Bien manger, c'est un luxe?

Une étude récente indique que certaines personnes dans notre société se nourrissent mal et mettent leur santé en danger.

Ces personnes dépensent moins de cinq euros par jour sur la nourriture. Et aujourd'hui une barre chocolatée et un paquet de chips coûtent moins cher qu'un morceau de fromage ou de viande.

Pour ces personnes il y a beaucoup de risques de santé: l'obésité, les problèmes de coeur, les cancers etc.

La solution? Le gouvernement doit fournir à ces gens des produits frais qui sont meilleurs pour la santé.

 et  ou  et  ?

Complete the sentences.

In France, some people eat badly and _____ in danger.

These people spend _____ per day on food.

The health risks are obesity, _____ and cancer.

The government should provide these people with _____ which are better for their health.

[Turn over

3. You read an article about helping airlines to trace lost luggage.

TRACEUR INTERNE

Placez à l'intérieur de votre bagage une étiquette portant votre nom, adresse et numéro de téléphone. Comme ça la compagnie aérienne peut retrouver le client quand l'étiquette extérieure a été arrachée.

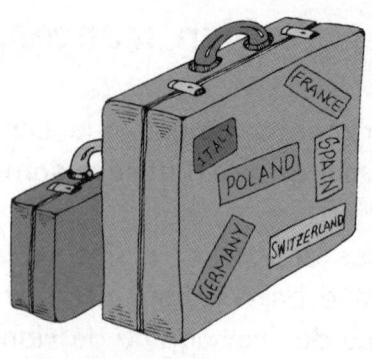

(a) What are you advised to put inside your luggage?

(b) When would this help the airline?

4. You read an advert about Toulouse airport.

www.toulouse.aeroport.fr

Nous vous souhaitons la bienvenue à bord de notre nouveau site Internet.

Il vous permet de choisir la meilleure offre, de réserver un vol à la dernière minute et de préparer un voyage d'affaires ou de loisirs . . .

On peut tout savoir sur l'aéroport Toulouse-Blagnac: les horaires, la location de voitures, et les tarifs des parkings par exemple.

Le monde aérien est à la portée de vos clics. Bon voyage!

(a) What services will this new Internet site provide? Mention any **two** things.

(b) What additional information can you find out about the airport? Mention any **two** things.

[Turn over

5. You read an article in which some French pupils give their opinions on school uniform.

Pour ou contre l'uniforme scolaire?

Je suis pour l'uniforme parce qu'il coûte moins cher que les vêtements à la mode, et les élèves travaillent mieux quand on porte l'uniforme.

Georges (Marseille)

Non à l'uniforme! J'ai horreur de porter une veste et une cravate en classe. Je veux choisir mes vêtements pour aller au collège.

Marcel (Bordeaux)

Moi, je suis absolument pour l'uniforme! Tout le monde s'habille de la même manière, donc il n'y a pas de distinction entre les élèves.

Adrienne (Paris)

Je dis "Non!" à l'uniforme au collège! Les vêtements qu'on porte font partie du caractère d'une personne. On doit être libre de s'exprimer comme on veut.

Estelle (Lyon)

Who says . . . ?

I want to choose my school clothes.	
Everyone dresses in the same way.	
A uniform costs less than fashionable clothes.	

6. Alain has written in to the magazine to complain about what he has to do at home.

Je m'occupe de tout à la maison

Pendant les grandes vacances je passe mes journées à la maison. En semaine, je dois surveiller ma petite soeur parce que mes parents sont tous les deux au travail.

Je dois aussi faire le ménage et préparer le repas du soir. Je n'ai pas un moment à moi. Que dois-je faire?

Alain, 16 ans

Tick (✓) **True** or **False** for each sentence.

	True	False
Alain has to look after his little sister at weekends.		
His parents are both out at work.		
Alain also has to do the gardening.		
He has to make the evening meal.		

[Turn over

7. Éric, the magazine's adviser, has written a reply to Alain.

> ### Il faut aider à la maison, mais . . .
>
> Je voudrais savoir combien d'heures par jour tu travailles à la maison.
>
> Il est normal que les adolescents aident un peu à la maison, comme par exemple faire leur lit, ranger leur chambre ou faire la vaisselle.
>
> Mais tes parents doivent comprendre que tu dois aussi avoir le temps de mener ta vie—pour faire du sport, pour écouter de la musique ou pour sortir avec tes amis.
>
> La solution? Tu dois discuter de cette question avec tes parents.
> Éric

Complete the sentences.

Éric wants to know _____ Alain works at home.

Éric thinks young people should make their bed, _____

or _____ .

Alain should also have time for doing sport, _____

or _____ .

8. You read an article about the "Famille Nombreuse" discount card which is available to families with more than two children.

LA CARTE FAMILLE NOMBREUSE

La carte "Famille Nombreuse" existe déjà: les familles avec plus de deux enfants bénéficient d'une réduction de tarif quand elles prennent le train.

A partir du mois de juillet la carte donnera aussi droit à des baisses de prix dans certains magasins d'électroménager et dans les piscines municipales. En 2009 on va voir aussi des auto-écoles, des compagnies d'assurances et des vendeurs d'automobiles sur la liste. Le gouvernement espère ainsi qu'un nombre important de familles nombreuses va profiter de la carte.

(a) At the moment, what is the benefit of using the "Famille Nombreuse" card?

(b) From July some places will offer price reductions. Mention any **one** place.

(c) Who will join the scheme in 2009? Mention any **one** group.

[Turn over

9. Michelle Dumoulin writes about her job as a flight attendant.

Hôtesse de l'air

Je travaille comme hôtesse de l'air depuis sept ans.

Après le baccalauréat*, j'ai dû faire une épreuve de langue anglaise pour la compagnie aérienne. Pour faire ce métier il faut parler très bien anglais.

Bien sûr, pendant les vols, je distribue les repas, je sers les boissons et je m'occupe du confort des passagers.

Mais j'ai aussi un rôle très important dans l'avion. En cas d'incidents, je dois rassurer les passagers et les aider à sortir de l'avion.

*le baccalauréat = school leaving examination

(a) After the baccalauréat, what did Michelle have to do to get the job? **1**

(b) What does Michelle do during flights? Mention any **two** things. **2**

(c) What does she have to do if there is an incident during a flight? Mention **two** things. **2**

Total (32)

[END OF QUESTION PAPER]

1000/407

NATIONAL
QUALIFICATIONS
2008

TUESDAY, 13 MAY
1.45 PM – 2.10 PM
(APPROX)

FRENCH
STANDARD GRADE
General Level
Listening Transcript

This paper must not be seen by any candidate.

The material overleaf is provided for use in an emergency only (eg the recording or equipment proving faulty) or where permission has been given in advance by SQA for the material to be read to candidates with additional support needs. The material must be read exactly as printed.

PB 1000/407 6/1010

GENERAL FRENCH 2008 — OFFICIAL SQA PAST PAPERS

Transcript—General Level

> **Instructions to reader(s):**
>
> For each item, read the English **once**, then read the French **three times**, with an interval of 5 seconds between the readings. On completion of the third reading, pause for the length of time indicated in brackets after each item, to allow the candidates to write their answers.
>
> Where special arrangements have been agreed in advance to allow the reading of the material, those sections marked **(f)** should be read by a female speaker and those marked **(m)** by a male: those sections marked **(t)** should be read by the teacher.

(t) You are spending a holiday with your family at a hotel in France.

(m) or (f) **Tu passes des vacances en famille dans un hôtel en France.**

(t) Question number one.

When you arrive the receptionist gives you some information. Where is your room? When do they start serving breakfast?

(m) **Alors, votre chambre est au deuxième étage. Le petit déjeuner est servi dans le restaurant à partir de sept heures et demie.**

(30 seconds)

(t) Question number two.

What else does he tell you?

Complete the sentences.

(m) **L'ascenseur est à droite. Il y a aussi une piscine pour les clients de l'hôtel. C'est gratuit.**

(30 seconds)

(t) Question number three.

The receptionist tells you there is a football match on Tuesday. How far away is the stadium?

(m) **Il y a un match de foot mardi soir. Le stade est à quinze minutes en voiture.**

(30 seconds)

(t) You meet Nicolas, a French boy who is also staying at the hotel with his family.

Question number four.

Where do Nicolas and his family live? Why do they come here for holidays?

(m) **Nous habitons à la campagne. Alors, passer les vacances au bord de la mer, c'est super.**

(30 seconds)

[1000/407] *Page two*

(t) **Question number five.**

Nicolas asks you two questions. What does he ask?

Tick **two** boxes.

(m) **C'est ta première visite dans cette région? Tu restes combien de temps ici?**

(*30 seconds*)

(t) **Question number six.**

Nicolas tells you what you can do there. What does he say?

Mention any **two** things.

(m) **On peut bronzer et faire de la planche à voile à la plage. Et, si tu aimes les chevaux, il y a un centre d'équitation.**

(*30 seconds*)

(t) **Question number seven.**

Nicolas talks about his sister. What does he say?

Tick **three** boxes.

(m) **Ma soeur est très contente d'être en vacances ici. Pendant les vacances de Pâques elle a travaillé dur pour ses examens. Elle veut aller à l'université au mois d'octobre. Mais pour le moment elle peut s'amuser.**

(*30 seconds*)

(t) **Question number eight.**

Nicolas talks about his parents. What does his father do? Mention any **one** thing.

Where does his mother work?

(m) **Mon père est propriétaire d'un magasin. Il vend des appareils électriques, par exemple des frigos et des machines à laver. Ma mère travaille dans l'Office de Tourisme dans notre ville.**

(*30 seconds*)

(t) **Question number nine.**

Nicolas' mother arrives and speaks to you. Why does she like coming here on holiday?

Mention any **two** things.

(f) **J'aime bien venir ici en vacances. Il y a beaucoup à faire pour les jeunes. Alors, je peux passer du temps avec mon mari parce que les enfants font toujours des activités avec leurs copains.**

(*30 seconds*)

[Turn over for Questions 10 to 12 on *Page four*

(t) **Question number ten.**

Nicolas makes a suggestion for the afternoon. What could you do? Mention any **one** thing.

Where and when does he suggest you meet?

(m) **Tu aimes le cyclisme? Alors, cet après-midi on peut louer des vélos et faire un tour de la ville. Rendez-vous devant l'hôtel après le déjeuner.**

(30 seconds)

(t) In the evening you eat in the hotel restaurant. Your waitress is a girl called Monique.

Question number eleven.

Monique tells you about herself. What does she say?

Tick **True** or **False** for each sentence.

(f) **Je suis née ici et mes parents habitent toujours dans cette ville. Je suis étudiante à l'université de Toulouse. Je rentre ici chez mes parents en été et je passe trois mois à travailler dans cet hôtel.**

(30 seconds)

(t) **Question number twelve.**

Monique talks about her future. What does she say?

Complete the sentences.

(f) **A l'université je fais des études d'informatique. L'année prochaine je vais faire un stage en Allemagne. Après mes études, j'espère développer de nouveaux programmes pour les ordinateurs.**

(30 seconds)

(t) End of test.

Now look over your answers.

[END OF TRANSCRIPT]

OFFICIAL SQA PAST PAPERS 19 GENERAL FRENCH 2008

FOR OFFICIAL USE

G

Total Mark

1000/406

NATIONAL QUALIFICATIONS 2008

TUESDAY, 13 MAY 1.45 PM – 2.10 PM (APPROX)

FRENCH STANDARD GRADE
General Level
Listening

Fill in these boxes and read what is printed below.

Full name of centre

Town

Forename(s)

Surname

Date of birth
Day Month Year

Scottish candidate number

Number of seat

When you are told to do so, open your paper.

You will hear a number of short items in French. You will hear each item three times, then you will have time to write your answer.

Write your answers, **in English**, in this book, in the appropriate spaces.

You may take notes as you are listening to the French, but only in this book.

You may **not** use a French dictionary.

You are not allowed to leave the examination room until the end of the test.

Before leaving the examination room you must give this book to the invigilator. If you do not, you may lose all the marks for this paper.

PB 1000/406 6/36070

You are spending a holiday with your family at a hotel in France.

Tu passes des vacances en famille dans un hôtel en France.

1. When you arrive the receptionist gives you some information.

    (a) Where is your room?

    _____

    (b) When do they start serving breakfast?

    _____

    * * * * *

2. What else does he tell you? Complete the sentences.

    The lift is _____ .

    For hotel customers the swimming pool is _____ .

    * * * * *

3. The receptionist tells you there is a football match on Tuesday. How far away is the stadium?

    _____

    * * * * *

You meet Nicolas, a French boy who is also staying at the hotel with his family.

4. (a) Where do Nicolas and his family live?

    _____

    (b) Why do they come here for holidays?

    _____

    * * * * *

5. Nicolas asks you two questions. What does he ask? Tick (✓) **two** boxes.

Is this your first visit to this area?	
Do you like this area?	
How long did your journey take?	
How long are you staying here?	

* * * * *

6. Nicolas tells you what you can do there. What does he say? Mention any **two** things.

_____

_____

* * * * *

7. Nicolas talks about his sister. What does he say? Tick (✓) **three** boxes.

His sister is happy to be on holiday.	
At Easter she went on holiday.	
At Easter she worked hard for her exams.	
She wants to go to university in England.	
She wants to go to university in October.	
She wants to get a job for the summer.	

* * * * *

[Turn over

8. Nicolas talks about his parents.

   (a) What does his father do? Mention any **one** thing.

   _____

   (b) Where does his mother work?

   _____

* * * * *

9. Nicolas' mother arrives and speaks to you.

   Why does she like coming here on holiday? Mention any **two** things.

   _____

   _____

* * * * *

10. Nicolas makes a suggestion for the afternoon.

   (a) What could you do? Mention any **one** thing.

   _____

   (b) Where and when does he suggest you meet?

   _____

* * * * *

In the evening you eat in the hotel restaurant. Your waitress is a girl called Monique.

11. Monique tells you about herself. What does she say? Tick (✓) **True** or **False** for each sentence.

	True	False
Monique's parents no longer live in the town.		
She has a holiday job in Toulouse.		
Each summer she works in the hotel for three months.		

* * * * *

12. Monique talks about her future. What does she say? Complete the sentences.

Monique is studying _____ at university.

Next year she is going to work _____ .

She hopes to get a job developing _____ .

* * * * *

Total (26)

[END OF QUESTION PAPER]

STANDARD GRADE | GENERAL
2009

OFFICIAL SQA PAST PAPERS 27 GENERAL FRENCH 2009

FOR OFFICIAL USE

Total

1000/402

NATIONAL
QUALIFICATIONS
2009

THURSDAY, 14 MAY
10.50 AM – 11.35 AM

FRENCH
STANDARD GRADE
General Level
Reading

Fill in these boxes and read what is printed below.

Full name of centre

Town

Forename(s)

Surname

Date of birth
Day Month Year

Scottish candidate number

Number of seat

When you are told to do so, open your paper and write your answers **in English** in the spaces provided.

You may use a French dictionary.

Before leaving the examination room you must give this book to the invigilator. If you do not, you may lose all the marks for this paper.

PB 1000/402 6/34820

You are reading a French magazine.

1. You see this article about school meals.

REPAS GRATUITS

La cantine est maintenant gratuite pour trois mille enfants dans certaines écoles primaires de Paris. Avant, beaucoup d'enfants n'allaient pas à la cantine à cause de problèmes financiers. Pour une famille de deux enfants cela représente une économie de 130€ par mois.

Complete the sentences.

The canteen is free for _____

in certain primary schools in Paris.

Lots of children didn't use the canteen before because of _____

_____.

A family with 2 children can save _____.

2. You then read an article which gives careers information.

INFO MÉTIER: JOURNALISTE

C'est un métier varié et important. Par exemple un journaliste pourrait présenter les informations à la télé, faire un reportage aux Etats-Unis, ou couvrir une rencontre sportive—on ne sait jamais.

Quelles sont les qualités d'un bon journaliste?

Il doit être curieux et savoir bien exprimer ses idées. En plus, il doit avoir de bons rapports avec les gens.

(a) Being a journalist can offer a lot of variety. Which tasks might be done? Mention any **two** things. 2

(b) What qualities should a journalist have? Mention any **two** things. 2

[Turn over

3. You then read an article about a British boy, Michael Perham.

BRAVO, MICHAEL!

A 14 ans, Michael Perham est le plus jeune navigateur à avoir traversé l'Atlantique en solitaire. Son papa le suivait en bateau à quelques kilomètres de distance. Pendant les 7 semaines de navigation, Michael a même trouvé le temps de faire ses devoirs!

Complete the sentences.

Michael Perham was the _____ sailor

to cross the Atlantic _____.

His father followed him by boat _____.

During the 7 weeks at sea Michael even found the time to _____

_____.

4. There is an interesting article about part-time jobs for teenagers.

COMMENT GAGNER DE L'ARGENT

En France, officiellement, on n'a pas le droit de travailler avant l'âge de 14 ans. Entre 14 et 16 ans, la loi est très stricte: on peut travailler seulement pendant les vacances scolaires, on ne peut pas travailler plus de la moitié des vacances et on a besoin d'une autorisation de l'Agence de l'Emploi.

Cependant, il est possible de recevoir de l'argent quand on rend des services à des voisins ou à sa famille. Par exemple, on peut garder les enfants, promener les chiens ou faire du jardinage.

In the grid below tick (✓) **True** or **False** beside each statement.

	True	False
In France you must be 14 before you can get a part-time job.		
14–16 year olds are allowed to work for more than half the school holidays.		
It is necessary to get permission from the Employment Office if you are under 16.		
You can only earn money doing jobs for your family.		
You are not allowed to look after children.		

[Turn over

5. You then read an article about music downloads.

LA MUSIQUE—ACHETER OU TÉLÉCHARGER?

Aujourd'hui, seuls les personnes riches ou les gens qui ont peur de télécharger* achètent leur musique dans un magasin. Par conséquent, c'est un gros problème pour les artistes car ils risquent de perdre beaucoup d'argent si le téléchargement vient d'un site illégal.

Récemment, on a proposé une solution: au début de chaque téléchargement, il y aura de la publicité qui va aider à rembourser les artistes.

* télécharger = to download

(a) According to the article, who are the only two groups of people who buy music in a shop? 2

(b) Downloading can cause a problem for performers. What is this problem? 1

(c) A solution has been suggested. What is going to happen at the beginning of each download? 1

6. You then read an article about advances in technology.

> **UN MONDE EN TRAIN DE CHANGER**
> Aujourd'hui, il est possible de reconnaître une personne en identifiant certaines parties de son corps: les empreintes des doigts et de la main, l'identification de la voix et de l'oeil. Dans quelques années, pour retirer de l'argent une carte bancaire ne sera pas essentielle. En plus, pour entrer dans la maison, pas besoin de clés! On placera la main sur un écran ou l'oeil devant une caméra.

(a) At the moment, how can people be identified? Mention any **two** things.   2

(b) What are we told about withdrawing money in the future?   1

(c) How will people get into their houses in the future? Mention any **one** thing.   1

[Turn over

7. You read the following letter in the magazine's problem page.

> **Chère Francine,**
>
> J'ai un bon copain mais il est pénible: il veut m'imiter tout le temps! Par exemple, quand je ris, il rit; il prend le même accent que moi pour raconter des blagues. Cela m'énerve beaucoup. Aidez-moi, s'il vous plaît.
>
> **Marc**

(a) Why has Marc written to the problem page?

(b) What behaviour does he mention in his example? Mention any **one** thing.

8. You read the reply to Marc's letter.

> **Cher Marc,**
> Il est évident que ton copain manque de confiance. Donc, il faut l'encourager à montrer sa propre personnalité.
> **Francine**

What does Francine say in her reply? Mention **two** things.

9. There is also an article about recycling.

LE RECYCLAGE

Depuis 2006, il ne faut pas jeter les équipements électroniques à la poubelle.

Pourtant, en France, très peu d'ordinateurs sont recyclés et ils contiennent plein de matériaux réutilisables . . . par exemple, il est possible de transformer le plastique en pneus, en cartes de crédit et en jouets.

Complete the sentences.

Since 2006 you are not allowed to _____

_____.

In France _____ computers are recycled.

It is possible to change plastic into _____,

credit cards and _____.

Total (32)

[END OF QUESTION PAPER]

1000/407

NATIONAL
QUALIFICATIONS
2009

THURSDAY, 14 MAY
11.55 AM – 12.20 PM
(APPROX)

FRENCH
STANDARD GRADE
General Level
Listening Transcript

This paper must not be seen by any candidate.

The material overleaf is provided for use in an emergency only (eg the recording or equipment proving faulty) or where permission has been given in advance by SQA for the material to be read to candidates with additional support needs. The material must be read exactly as printed.

Transcript—General Level

> **Instructions to reader(s):**
>
> For each item, read the English **once**, then read the French **three times**, with an interval of 5 seconds between the readings. On completion of the third reading, pause for the length of time indicated in brackets after each item, to allow the candidates to write their answers.
>
> Where special arrangements have been agreed in advance to allow the reading of the material, those sections marked **(f)** should be read by a female speaker and those marked **(m)** by a male; those sections marked **(t)** should be read by the teacher.

(t) You are travelling to France on a school trip.

(m) or (f) Tu fais un voyage en France en groupe scolaire.

(t) Question number one.

On the way to your hotel you listen to the radio. You hear the weather forecast. What does it say? Mention any **one** thing.

(m) or (f) Salut à tous. Aujourd'hui, un temps magnifique dans toute la région. Température vingt-cinq degrés.

(30 seconds)

(t) Question number two.

You hear an advert for a new supermarket. What details are you given?

Complete the sentence.

(m) or (f) Venez visiter le nouveau supermarché "EXTRA". Ouvert entre sept heures et vingt-deux heures. Les cent premiers clients vont recevoir une boîte de chocolats!

(30 seconds)

(t) Question number three.

You then hear a news flash about an accident. Where did the accident take place? Why is the road blocked?

(m) or (f) Il y a eu un accident près de la gare. La route est bloquée pour le moment parce que trois voitures sont entrées en collision.

(30 seconds)

(t) Question number four.

You hear details of a competition. What prize is being offered? What is the question you have to answer?

(m) or (f) Pour gagner un téléphone portable répondez à la question suivante . . . Comment s'appelle le Président de la France?

(30 seconds)

(t) **Question number five.**

You arrive at your hotel and the owner welcomes you. What does he ask you?

(m) **Bienvenue à l'Hôtel Bellevue. Vous avez fait un bon voyage?**

(*30 seconds*)

(t) **Question number six.**

He speaks to your group about some of the hotel rules. What are they?

Complete the sentences.

(m) **Tout d'abord, il y a quelques règles à respecter. Il est interdit de manger dans les chambres et on ne doit pas prendre de douche après onze heures du soir.**

(*30 seconds*)

(t) **Question number seven.**

The owner tells you about some of the facilities in the hotel. What is available?

Mention **two** things.

(m) **Dans l'hôtel nous avons une petite salle de jeux et des courts de tennis.**

(*30 seconds*)

(t) **Question number eight.**

He goes on to tell you about what there is to do in the area. What does he say?

Mention **two** things.

(m) **Il y a plusieurs sites historiques à visiter dans la région. Vous avez aussi la possibilité d'aller au parc d'attractions.**

(*30 seconds*)

(t) **Question number nine.**

Later you meet a French girl, Nathalie, who is staying at the hotel with a group from her school. What does she ask you?

Tick the **two** correct boxes.

(f) **Tu as déjà visité la France? Tu restes combien de temps ici?**

(*30 seconds*)

(t) **Question number ten.**

She tells you about her school. What does she say?

Mention any **one** thing.

(f) **Notre collège est situé dans le nord-ouest de la France. Il est très vieux.**

(*30 seconds*)

[*Turn over for Questions 11 to 13 on* Page four

(t) Question number eleven.

Nathalie gives her opinion about history and maths. What does she think of each subject and why?

Complete the grid.

(f) **Ma matière préférée c'est l'histoire car le prof est jeune. Par contre, j'ai horreur des maths parce que les leçons sont ennuyeuses.**

(30 seconds)

(t) Question number twelve.

Nathalie tells you what she will be doing tomorrow with her school group.

Tick **True** or **False** for each sentence.

(f) **Demain matin on va au marché qui se trouve devant la mairie. J'espère acheter un souvenir pour ma meilleure amie. L'après-midi nous allons visiter un château du dix-huitième siècle.**

(30 seconds)

(t) Question number thirteen.

Why does Nathalie have to leave?

Mention **two** things.

(f) **Je dois partir maintenant. Notre groupe va faire un tour de la ville et on part dans quinze minutes.**

(30 seconds)

(t) End of test.

Now look over your answers.

[END OF TRANSCRIPT]

OFFICIAL SQA PAST PAPERS   41   GENERAL FRENCH 2009

FOR OFFICIAL USE

G

Total Mark

1000/406

NATIONAL QUALIFICATIONS 2009

THURSDAY, 14 MAY 11.55 AM – 12.20 PM (APPROX)

FRENCH
STANDARD GRADE
General Level
Listening

Fill in these boxes and read what is printed below.

Full name of centre

Town

Forename(s)

Surname

Date of birth
Day Month Year

Scottish candidate number

Number of seat

When you are told to do so, open your paper.

You will hear a number of short items in French. You will hear each item three times, then you will have time to write your answer.

Write your answers, **in English**, in this book, in the appropriate spaces.

You may take notes as you are listening to the French, but only in this book.

You may **not** use a French dictionary.

You are not allowed to leave the examination room until the end of the test.

Before leaving the examination room you must give this book to the invigilator. If you do not, you may lose all the marks for this paper.

SQA

PB 1000/406   6/34820

You are travelling to France on a school trip.

Tu fais un voyage en France en groupe scolaire.

1. On the way to your hotel you listen to the radio. You hear the weather forecast. What does it say? Mention any **one** thing.

   _____

   * * * * *

2. You hear an advert for a new supermarket. What details are you given? Complete the sentence.

   Come and visit "EXTRA" the new supermarket. Open between 7 am and 10 pm. The first _____ customers will receive a _____.

   * * * * *

3. You then hear a news flash about an accident.

   (a) Where did the accident take place?

   _____

   (b) Why is the road blocked?

   _____

   * * * * *

4. You hear details of a competition.

   (a) What prize is being offered?

   _____

   (b) What is the question you have to answer?

   _____

   * * * * *

5. You arrive at your hotel and the owner welcomes you. What does he ask you?

_____

* * * * *

6. He speaks to your group about some of the hotel rules. What are they? Complete the sentences.

You are not allowed to _____.

You must not_____ after 11 pm.

* * * * *

7. The owner tells you about some of the facilities in the hotel. What is available? Mention **two** things.

_____

_____

* * * * *

8. He goes on to tell you about what there is to do in the area. What does he say? Mention **two** things.

_____

_____

* * * * *

9. Later you meet a French girl, Nathalie, who is staying at the hotel with a group from her school. What does she ask you? Tick (✓) the **two** correct boxes.

Do you like coming to France?	
Have you visited France before?	
How long will you be staying here?	
How long was your journey here?	

* * * * *

[Turn over for Questions 10 to 13 on *Page four*

10. She tells you about her school. What does she say? Mention any **one** thing.

_____

* * * * *

11. Nathalie gives her opinion about history and maths. What does she think of each subject and why? Complete the grid.

	Opinion	Reason
History		
Maths		

* * * * *

12. Nathalie tells you what she will be doing tomorrow with her school group. Tick (✓) **True** or **False** for each sentence.

	True	False
There is a market behind the town hall.		
Nathalie hopes to buy a souvenir for her best friend.		
They are going to visit a seventeenth-century castle.		

* * * * *

13. Why does Nathalie have to leave? Mention **two** things.

_____

_____

* * * * *

Total (26)

[END OF QUESTION PAPER]

STANDARD GRADE | GENERAL
2010

OFFICIAL SQA PAST PAPERS 47 GENERAL FRENCH 2010

FOR OFFICIAL USE

G

Total

1000/402

NATIONAL
QUALIFICATIONS
2010

TUESDAY, 11 MAY
10.50 AM – 11.35 AM

**FRENCH
STANDARD GRADE**
General Level
Reading

Fill in these boxes and read what is printed below.

Full name of centre

Town

Forename(s)

Surname

Date of birth
Day Month Year   Scottish candidate number   Number of seat

When you are told to do so, open your paper and write your answers **in English** in the spaces provided.

You may use a French dictionary.

Before leaving the examination room you must give this book to the Invigilator. If you do not, you may lose all the marks for this paper.

SQA

PB 1000/402 6/33810

1. You read an interview in a French magazine about the actress Hafsia Herzi.

> **ÉVÉNEMENT CINÉMA**
>
> **Interview avec Hafsia Herzi**
>
> *Tu étais comment comme adolescente?*
>
> J'adorais le collège, les cours, les copines. J'étais toujours une élève travailleuse, avec des rêves de cinéma.
>
> *As-tu des conseils à donner aux jeunes qui voudraient devenir acteur/actrice?*
>
> Il faut avoir de la confiance et bien travailler à l'école. Ce n'est pas un métier facile parce qu'il y a beaucoup de personnes qui voudraient être célèbres.
>
> *Tu prenais des cours de théâtre?*
>
> Non, quand j'étais jeune, mes parents n'avaient pas assez d'argent. Donc ce n'était pas possible.

(a) What was Hafsia like as a teenager? Tick (✓) the **two** correct boxes. **2**

She was a hardworking pupil.	
She was a lazy pupil.	
She dreamed of the cinema.	
She worked in the cinema.	

(b) What advice does she have for other teenagers who want to act? Mention any **two** things. **2**

_____

_____

(c) Why did she not take acting lessons? **1**

_____

2. There is also an article giving advice on preparing for exams.

> **La bonne méthode pour réviser**
>
> **Il y a des choses que vous ne comprenez pas?**
>
> - Ne paniquez pas
> - Demandez de l'aide à votre prof
> - Cherchez des explications dans vos livres
>
> **Pour bien mémoriser les dates, on recommande les techniques suivantes:**
>
> - Répétez les dates à voix haute
> - Ecrivez les dates plusieurs fois
> - Demandez à vos copains de vous poser des questions sur les dates.

(a) If you don't understand something, what should you do? Mention any **one** thing. **1**

(b) What can you do to help memorise dates? Mention any **two** things. **2**

[Turn over

3. You read some more advice on exam preparation.

La préparation physique

Dans les jours avant un examen une bonne préparation physique est vraiment nécessaire.

On doit avoir un minimum de huit heures de sommeil chaque nuit.

Mangez équilibré—oubliez le régime. Prenez le temps de bien manger.

Pratiquez une activité physique tous les jours.

What should you do to be in good physical condition before an exam? Mention any **two** things.

2

4. On the next page, there is an article about a young boy who lives on a farm.

> Je me lève très tôt le matin parce que je dois aider mon père avec les vaches.
>
> J'aime bien être dehors quand le soleil se lève—c'est magnifique!
>
> Quand on rentre à sept heures pour manger le petit déjeuner j'ai toujours très faim. J'adore boire le chocolat chaud que ma mère prépare pour moi.

Complete the following sentences.

I _____ in the morning because I have to _____ with the cows.

I really like _____ when the sun rises—it's magnificent!

When we come in at 7 am to have our breakfast, I am _____.

[Turn over

5. The article continues.

> Je ne veux pas me lever si tôt mais voilà comment je gagne mon argent de poche.
>
> Avec mon argent je dois faire des économies pour mes prochaines vacances. Mais ce n'est pas toujours facile parce que je suis vraiment dépensier! J'aime bien sortir avec mes amis, traîner dans les cafés ou bien acheter plein de vêtements à la mode.

What does he say about pocket money? Tick (✓) the **two** correct boxes.

He saves up for presents.	
He finds it easy to save.	
He goes out with his friends.	
He buys fashionable clothes.	

6. You pick up a holiday brochure which catches your eye.

> **Multiactivités à la carte ou détente à Val Cenis**
>
> **Pour les amateurs de VTT*:** on propose un stage de huit jours en pleine montagne.
>
> **Un week-end de randonnée pédestre**: profitez d'une randonnée à pied accompagnée d'un guide expérimenté. Vous logez dans une auberge de jeunesse.
>
> **Escalade**: Tout le matériel nécessaire est fourni pour le week-end.
>
> *VTT = vélo tout terrain

(a) What is available for those interested in mountain biking? **1**

(b) What are we told about the hiking weekend? Mention any **one** thing. **1**

(c) What are we told about the climbing weekend? **1**

[Turn over

7. You get more information about this holiday in the mountains.

Hébergement en haute montagne, qui bénéficie d'une vue magnifique. Il y a aussi plein d'activités sportives pour les jeunes. C'est un endroit idéal pour les gens qui aiment les vacances actives en plein air!

What are you told? Mention any **two** things.

8. You also look at a brochure which is advertising a weekend deal in Paris.

> **Paris—capitale de mille et une facettes**
>
> Le prix de votre séjour comprend:
>
> - Trois nuits, petit déjeuner compris
> - Un ticket qui permet les voyages sans limite dans les transports en commun
> - Entrée gratuite aux musées
> - Une croisière sur la Seine.

What does the price include? Mention any **three** things.

[Turn over

9. You pick up a brochure which advises elderly people what to do during a heatwave.

QUELQUES CONSEILS POUR LES PERSONNES ÂGÉES PENDANT LA CANICULE

- Il ne faut pas sortir aux heures les plus chaudes
- Il est recommandé de boire environ 1,5 L d'eau par jour
- On devrait passer plusieurs heures dans un endroit climatisé

What advice is given? Complete the sentences.

You shouldn't go out _____.

You should drink _____.

You should spend several hours in _____.

10. You find an interesting article about personal hygiene in France through the years.

Saviez-vous que . . . ?

Pendant le Moyen Age
Les gens ne se lavaient pas les cheveux—généralement on se coupait les cheveux courts.

Pendant le 17ᵉ et 18ᵉ siècles
A la cour de Louis XVI, on se poudrait et on se parfumait pour cacher les odeurs.

A la fin du 19ᵉ siècle l'eau courante est installée et on commençait à prendre les bains régulièrement.

Aujourd'hui
95% des foyers français sont équipés d'une douche.
3% des Français n'utilisent pas de brosse à dents.

Complete the sentences.

In the Middle Ages, people didn't wash their hair. Generally, they _____.

At the court of Louis XVI they used powder and perfume to _____.

At the end of the 19th century running water was installed and people started to _____.

Today, 95% of French homes _____.

3% of French people _____ a toothbrush.

Total (32)

[END OF QUESTION PAPER]

1000/407

NATIONAL
QUALIFICATIONS
2010

TUESDAY, 11 MAY
11.55 AM – 12.20 PM
(APPROX)

FRENCH
STANDARD GRADE
General Level
Listening Transcript

This paper must not be seen by any candidate.

The material overleaf is provided for use in an emergency only (eg the recording or equipment proving faulty) or where permission has been given in advance by SQA for the material to be read to candidates with additional support needs. The material must be read exactly as printed.

Transcript—General Level

> **Instructions to reader(s):**
>
> For each item, read the English **once**, then read the French **three times**, with an interval of 5 seconds between the readings. On completion of the third reading, pause for the length of time indicated in brackets after each item, to allow the candidates to write their answers.
>
> Where special arrangements have been agreed in advance to allow the reading of the material, those sections marked **(f)** should be read by a female speaker and those marked **(m)** by a male; those sections marked **(t)** should be read by the teacher.

(t) You are on holiday in France with your family and you arrive at your hotel.

(m) or (f) **Tu passes les vacances en France avec ta famille et vous arrivez à votre hôtel.**

(t) **Question number one.**

The receptionist speaks to you. What does she ask for? Mention **two** things.

(f) **Bonjour, messieurs dames. Vous avez votre lettre de réservation et une pièce d'identité, s'il vous plaît?**

(30 seconds)

(t) **Question number two.**

She gives you some more information about breakfast. What does she say? Complete the sentences.

(f) **Le petit déjeuner est servi entre sept heures et neuf heures trente. C'est en libre service.**

(30 seconds)

(t) **Question number three.**

She tells you about the bedrooms. Where are they? Mention **two** things.

(f) **Voici les clés. Les chambres sont au troisième étage, en face de l'ascenseur.**

(30 seconds)

(t) **Question number four.**

Later, you go down to the games room where you meet Olivier, a French teenager. He asks you some questions. What does he say? Tick **two** boxes.

(m) **Quand es-tu arrivé?**
Tu passes combien de temps ici?

(30 seconds)

(t) Question number five.

Olivier tells you about where he lives in France. What does he say? Tick **True** or **False** for each statement.

(m) **Moi, je viens d'une ville industrielle dans le nord de la France. C'est grand comme ville. Il y a cinquante mille habitants.**

(30 seconds)

(t) Question number six.

He goes on to say what he thinks of his town. What does he say? Mention any **two** things.

(m) **Là, où j'habite . . . je n'aime pas tellement. Il y a beaucoup de voitures dans les rues et c'est pollué.**

(30 seconds)

(t) Question number seven.

He tells you why he and his family are spending their holidays in this area. What does he say his parents like? Mention any **two** things.

(m) **Chaque année on passe les vacances au bord de la mer. Mes parents adorent bronzer, faire de longues promenades sur la plage ou bien faire des sports nautiques.**

(30 seconds)

(t) Question number eight.

Olivier introduces you to his older sister Sandrine. What does he say about her? Mention **two** things.

(m) **Voici ma sœur aînée, Sandrine. Elle est étudiante à l'université de Lyon. Elle va être professeur d'histoire.**

(30 seconds)

(t) Question number nine.

Sandrine tells you that she has been to Scotland. What does she say about her visit? Complete the sentences.

(f) **Quand j'avais onze ans je suis allée en Ecosse en groupe scolaire. J'ai beaucoup aimé le château d'Edimbourg et les belles montagnes.**

(30 seconds)

(t) Question number ten.

Sandrine tells you about the local market.

When does it take place? Where is it situated?

(f) **Mercredi matin on va au marché qui se trouve sur la place devant la mairie.**

(30 seconds)

[*Turn over for Questions 11 and 12 on* Page four

(t) Question number eleven.

She tells you what souvenirs she hopes to buy there. What is she going to buy?

(f) Je voudrais acheter des souvenirs: des lunettes de soleil pour mon copain et une bouteille de vin pour mon grand-père.

(30 seconds)

(t) Question number twelve.

Olivier tells you about a disco organised for later that evening. Why is he going?

(m) Il y a une disco ce soir à neuf heures. J'y vais parce que c'est gratuit.

(30 seconds)

(t) End of test.

Now look over your answers.

[END OF TRANSCRIPT]

OFFICIAL SQA PAST PAPERS 63 GENERAL FRENCH 2010

FOR OFFICIAL USE

G

Total Mark

1000/406

NATIONAL QUALIFICATIONS 2010

TUESDAY, 11 MAY 11.55 AM – 12.20 PM (APPROX)

FRENCH STANDARD GRADE
General Level
Listening

Fill in these boxes and read what is printed below.

Full name of centre

Town

Forename(s)

Surname

Date of birth

Day Month Year   Scottish candidate number   Number of seat

When you are told to do so, open your paper.

You will hear a number of short items in French. You will hear each item three times, then you will have time to write your answer.

Write your answers, **in English**, in this book, in the appropriate spaces.

You may take notes as you are listening to the French, but only in this book.

You may **not** use a French dictionary.

You are not allowed to leave the examination room until the end of the test.

Before leaving the examination room you must give this book to the Invigilator. If you do not, you may lose all the marks for this paper.

PB 1000/406 6/33810

SQA

You are on holiday in France with your family and you arrive at your hotel.

Tu passes les vacances en France avec ta famille et vous arrivez à votre hôtel.

1. The receptionist speaks to you. What does she ask for? Mention **two** things.

   _____
   _____

   * * * * *

2. She gives you some more information about breakfast. What does she say? Complete the sentences.

   Breakfast is served between _____ and _____.

   It is _____.

   * * * * *

3. She tells you about the bedrooms. Where are they? Mention **two** things.

   _____
   _____

   * * * * *

4. Later, you go down to the games room where you meet Olivier, a French teenager. He asks you some questions. What does he say? Tick (✓) **two** boxes.

When did you arrive?	
Are you tired?	
How was your journey?	
How long are you staying here?	

   * * * * *

5. Olivier tells you about where he lives in France. What does he say? Tick (✓) **True** or **False** for each statement.

	True	False
I live in an industrial town.		
It's in the west of France.		
Fifty thousand people live there.		

Marks: 3

* * * * *

6. He goes on to say what he thinks of his town. What does he say? Mention any **two** things.

_____

_____

Marks: 2

* * * * *

7. He tells you why he and his family are spending their holidays in this area. What does he say his parents like? Mention any **two** things.

_____

_____

Marks: 2

* * * * *

8. Olivier introduces you to his older sister Sandrine. What does he say about her? Mention **two** things.

_____

_____

Marks: 2

* * * * *

[Turn over for Questions 9 to 12 on *Page four*

Marks

9. Sandrine tells you that she has been to Scotland. What does she say about her visit? Complete the sentences.

   When I was eleven, I went to Scotland _____.

   I really liked _____ and

   _____.

   3

   * * * * *

10. Sandrine tells you about the local market.

    (a) When does it take place?

    _____

    1

    (b) Where is it situated?

    _____

    1

    * * * * *

11. She tells you what souvenirs she hopes to buy there. What is she going to buy?

For her friend	
For her grandad	

    2

    * * * * *

12. Olivier tells you about a disco organised for later that evening. Why is he going?

    _____

    1

    * * * * *

   Total (26)

   [END OF QUESTION PAPER]

STANDARD GRADE | GENERAL

2011

OFFICIAL SQA PAST PAPERS   69   GENERAL FRENCH 2011

FOR OFFICIAL USE

G

Total

1000/402

NATIONAL QUALIFICATIONS 2011

WEDNESDAY, 11 MAY 10.50 AM – 11.35 AM

FRENCH
STANDARD GRADE
General Level
Reading

Fill in these boxes and read what is printed below.

Full name of centre

Town

Forename(s)

Surname

Date of birth

Day   Month   Year   Scottish candidate number   Number of seat

When you are told to do so, open your paper and write your answers **in English** in the spaces provided.

You may use a French dictionary.

Before leaving the examination room you must give this book to the Invigilator. If you do not, you may lose all the marks for this paper.

SQA

PB 1000/402 6/28810

You are reading a French magazine.

1. There is an article about what teenagers think of their home area.

> Moi, j'habite le nord-est de la France. Dans ma région qui s'appelle l'Alsace, il y a beaucoup de montagnes où j'aime bien faire du ski et faire des randonnées. C'est pratique parce que les stations de sports d'hiver ne sont pas très loin.
>
> **LAURIANE**

Complete the sentences.

Lauriane likes skiing and _____.

It's handy because the ski resorts are _____.

2. The article continues.

> Moi, je viens de Quimper, en Bretagne. Je suis fier de ma région parce qu'on a sa propre langue qui s'appelle le breton, et il y a des festivals de musique traditionnelle.
>
> **BRIEUC**

Complete the sentence.

Brieuc is proud of his area because it has _____

and there are _____.

[Turn over

3. You see this letter on the problem page.

> Je préfère passer mon temps libre avec les copains—on parle de tout et on rigole. A la maison c'est bien différent parce que je ne suis jamais tranquille à cause de ma petite sœur. Elle m'énerve, par exemple, quand je travaille à l'ordinateur ou quand je lis dans ma chambre.
>
> **CHRISTOPHE**

(a) What does Christophe do when he is with his friends? Mention any **two** things.

2

(b) At home, when does his sister annoy him? Mention **two** things.

2

4. An article in the magazine is giving advice on organising a party.

> **LE CODE DU BON FÊTARD**
>
> Tu organises ta première fête et cela te stresse? Pas de panique. Voici quelques conseils pour t'aider . . .
>
> - Organise un espace vide avec les chaises contre les murs.
> - Choisis de la vaisselle en plastique.
> - Demande à tes parents de quitter la maison mais de rester en contact en cas de problème.
> - N'oublie pas d'informer tes voisins de la fête!
> - Prépare des activités au cas où personne ne danse.

Complete the sentences.

- Prepare an empty space with _____.

- Choose _____.

- Ask your parents to leave the house but to _____
  _____.

- Don't forget to _____.

- Prepare activities in case _____.

[Turn over

5. You then read an article about robots.

LES ROBOTS

De nos jours les robots existent partout. Les robots industriels sont employés dans les hôpitaux, dans les usines, et par l'armée. Ils font des tâches qui sont répétitives, dangereuses ou pénibles.

Dans la maison les robots rendent service pour la cuisine et le ménage. Les robots domestiques les plus populaires sont les aspirateurs qui nettoient tout seuls.

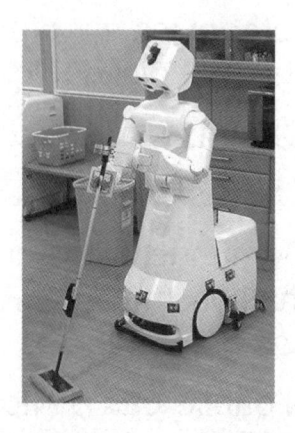

(a) Apart from hospitals, where are industrial robots used? Mention any **one** thing. 1

(b) What sort of tasks do these robots do? Mention any **one** thing. 1

(c) What services do robots provide in the home? Mention any **one** thing. 1

(d) Which type of domestic robots are the most popular? 1

6. You read an article about teenagers in three different parts of the world.

FRANCE

Une famille sur deux possède un ordinateur. Avec la télé, l'ordinateur et les jeux vidéo les adolescents passent en moyenne quatre heures par jour devant un écran.

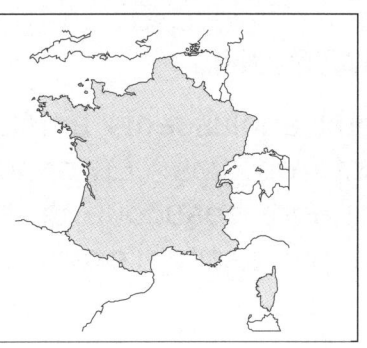

Complete the sentence.

In France, teenagers spend on average _____

in front of a screen.

[Turn over

7. The article continues.

ETATS-UNIS

Deux adolescents américains sur cinq sont trop gros. En général, les jeunes mangent beaucoup de sucreries et ne font pas assez d'exercice.

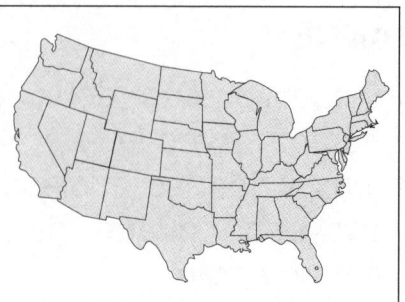

Complete the sentences.

In the USA, two teenagers in five are _____.

In general young people _____

and they don't _____.

8. The article continues.

> **MOYEN-ORIENT**
>
> Dans quelques pays une fille sur deux ne va pas à l'école. Voilà pourquoi . . . les filles se marient jeunes et elles ont des enfants très tôt. Donc, elles ne finissent pas leurs études.

Complete the sentences.

In some countries in the Middle East, one girl in two _____

_____ .

This is because girls _____

and don't _____ .

[Turn over

9. You read an article about a chef called Alex who works in a hotel.

CHEF DE CUISINE

Mon emploi est aussi ma passion. Je suis responsable de la carte du restaurant et du service en chambre. En plus, je dois créer des menus spéciaux pour Noël et le jour de l'an . . . On travaille en équipe et chaque semaine je demande à tous les autres cuisiniers de préparer de nouveaux plats. Moi, je goûte tous ces plats personnellement et, si je les aime, je les ajoute à la carte. C'est un métier où on travaille dur et où il n'y a pas d'heures fixes.

(a) What is Alex responsible for? Mention any **one** thing.

(b) Why does he mention Christmas Day and New Year's Day?

(c) What does he ask his team of cooks to do each week?

(d) What does Alex then do? Mention any **one** thing.

(e) What does he say about his job? Mention any **one** thing.

10. You read about two special dates in France.

LES FÊTES

Le 1er et le 8 mai sont deux dates spéciales en France. Ce sont des jours importants dans l'histoire du pays et ces jours-là on ne va ni au collège, ni au travail.

Le 1er mai, c'est la Fête du travail. Au 19ième siècle, les ouvriers manifestaient le 1er mai parce qu'ils voulaient limiter la durée du travail à huit heures par jour.

Le 8 mai on commémore la fin de la Seconde Guerre mondiale en 1945. C'est le jour où on honore la mémoire des soldats morts pour la France.

(a) The 1st and 8th of May are two special dates in France. What are we told about them? Mention any **one** thing. **1**

(b) In the nineteenth century workers held demonstrations on the 1st May. Why did they demonstrate? **1**

(c) Whose memory is honoured on the 8th of May? **1**

Total (32)

[END OF QUESTION PAPER]

1000/407

NATIONAL
QUALIFICATIONS
2011

WEDNESDAY, 11 MAY
11.55 AM – 12.20 PM
(APPROX)

FRENCH
STANDARD GRADE
General Level
Listening Transcript

This paper must not be seen by any candidate.

The material overleaf is provided for use in an emergency only (eg the recording or equipment proving faulty) or where permission has been given in advance by SQA for the material to be read to candidates with additional support needs. The material must be read exactly as printed.

Transcript—General Level

> **Instructions to reader(s):**
>
> For each item, read the English **once**, then read the French **three times**, with an interval of 5 seconds between the readings. On completion of the third reading, pause for the length of time indicated in brackets after each item, to allow the candidates to write their answers.
>
> Where special arrangements have been agreed in advance to allow the reading of the material, those sections marked **(f)** should be read by a female speaker and those marked **(m)** by a male; those sections marked **(t)** should be read by the teacher.

(t) While on holiday at your French friend's house, you are listening to a local French radio programme which includes interviews with young people.

(m) or (f) En vacances chez ton ami français, tu écoutes une émission à la radio régionale où il y a des interviews avec des jeunes.

(t) Question number one.

They are discussing the idea of school uniform. What does Paul say? Complete the sentence.

(m) **L'uniforme ce n'est pas pour moi!**

(30 seconds)

(t) Question number two.

Marie gives her opinion. What does she say? Mention any **one** thing.

(f) **Les uniformes coûtent très cher. C'est difficile pour les grandes familles.**

(30 seconds)

(t) Question number three.

What does Marie say about her life at school? Tick **two** boxes.

(f) **Mon collège est très vieux et les profs sont ennuyeux. Mais ma matière préférée est l'anglais parce que ma prof est sympa.**

(30 seconds)

(t) Question number four.

What does she say about what there is in her area? Complete the sentences.

(f) **Ma région fait beaucoup pour les jeunes. Il y a une piscine en plein air et des terrains de foot.**

(30 seconds)

(t) **Question number five.**

Paul tells you what he likes to do at the weekend. What does he say? Mention any **two** things.

(m) Le weekend j'adore promener mon petit chien. En plus, je bavarde avec mes copains ou bien je regarde un match de foot au stade.

(30 seconds)

(t) **Question number six.**

Marie talks about how she earns her pocket money. What does she have to do? Mention any **two** things.

(f) Pour gagner mon argent de poche, je dois laver la voiture, mettre la table chaque soir et ranger ma chambre.

(30 seconds)

(t) **Question number seven.**

Paul talks about what he does to earn money. What does he say? Tick **True** or **False** for each sentence.

(m) Moi, j'ai un petit job. Je travaille le samedi dans le bureau de mon oncle. J'aide à répondre au téléphone et je prépare le café pour tout le monde le matin.

(30 seconds)

(t) **Question number eight.**

Marie talks about how she spends her money. What does she spend it on? Mention **two** things.

(f) Je dois payer le bus pour aller en ville tous les week-ends et parfois j'achète des vêtements.

(30 seconds)

(t) **Question number nine.**

On the radio programme there is a competition. What is the prize? What is the question you have to answer?

(f) or (m) Attention! Vous voulez gagner des billets pour le concert ce soir? C'est simple! Répondez à cette petite question: quelle est la capitale de l'Espagne?

(30 seconds)

(t) **Question number ten.**

The radio presenter is talking about a show that is taking place in the town today. How would you get there? Complete the sentence.

(f) or (m) Quand vouz arrivez à la gare, vous tournez à droite et c'est la troisième rue à gauche, après le pont.

(30 seconds)

[*Turn over for Questions 11, 12 and 13 on* Page four

(t) Question number eleven.

The weather forecast is next. What will the weather be like tomorrow? Mention any **two** things.

(f) or (m) Demain, ce sera un jour magnifique avec quelques nuages et il va faire vingt-neuf degrés.

(*30 seconds*)

(t) Question number twelve.

You then hear an advertisement for a new restaurant. When does it open? What is the special offer?

(f) or (m) Le nouveau restaurant Chez Marc ouvre samedi prochain! Si vous êtes un groupe de quatre personnes vous payez seulement pour trois!

(*30 seconds*)

(t) Question number thirteen.

What other information is given? Complete the sentences.

(f) or (m) Il faut réserver à l'avance. Pour tous renseignements téléphonez au 06–82–02–25–85.

(*30 seconds*)

(t) End of test.

Now look over your answers.

[*END OF TRANSCRIPT*]

OFFICIAL SQA PAST PAPERS   85   GENERAL FRENCH 2011

FOR OFFICIAL USE

Total Mark

G

1000/406

NATIONAL
QUALIFICATIONS
2011

WEDNESDAY, 11 MAY
11.55 AM – 12.20 PM
(APPROX)

FRENCH
STANDARD GRADE
General Level
Listening

Fill in these boxes and read what is printed below.

Full name of centre

Town

Forename(s)

Surname

Date of birth

Day   Month   Year   Scottish candidate number   Number of seat

When you are told to do so, open your paper.

You will hear a number of short items in French. You will hear each item three times, then you will have time to write your answer.

Write your answers, **in English**, in this book, in the appropriate spaces.

You may take notes as you are listening to the French, but only in this book.

You may **not** use a French dictionary.

You are not allowed to leave the examination room until the end of the test.

Before leaving the examination room you must give this book to the Invigilator. If you do not, you may lose all the marks for this paper.

SQA

PB 1000/406 6/28810

While on holiday at your French friend's house, you are listening to a local French radio programme which includes interviews with young people.

En vacances chez ton ami français, tu écoutes une émission à la radio régionale où il y a des interviews avec des jeunes.

1. They are discussing the idea of school uniform. What does Paul say? Complete the sentence.

Uniform is _____.

* * * * *

2. Marie gives her opinion. What does she say? Mention any **one** thing.

_____

* * * * *

3. What does Marie say about her life at school? Tick (✓) **two** boxes.

The school is old.	
The school is boring.	
She hates English.	
Her English teacher is nice.	

* * * * *

4. What does she say about what there is in her area? Complete the sentences.

My area has lots for _____.

There is an _____ swimming pool and football pitches.

* * * * *

5. Paul tells you what he likes to do at the weekend. What does he say? Mention any **two** things.

_____
_____

* * * * *

[1000/406] Page two

6. Marie talks about how she earns her pocket money. What does she have to do? Mention any **two** things.

2

* * * * *

7. Paul talks about what he does to earn money. What does he say? Tick (✓) **True** or **False** for each sentence.

3

	True	False
He works on Saturday.		
He works in his uncle's shop.		
He makes the coffee in the afternoon.		

* * * * *

8. Marie talks about how she spends her money. What does she spend it on? Mention **two** things.

2

* * * * *

9. On the radio programme there is a competition.

(a) What is the prize?

1

(b) What is the question you have to answer?

1

[Turn over for Questions 10 to 13 on *Page four*

Page three

10. The radio presenter is talking about a show that is taking place in the town today. How would you get there? Complete the sentence.   **3**

When you arrive at _____ you turn _____

and it's the _____ on your left, after the bridge.

* * * * *

11. The weather forecast is next. What will the weather be like tomorrow? Mention any **two** things.   **2**

_____

_____

* * * * *

12. You then hear an advertisement for a new restaurant.

(a) When does it open?   **1**

_____

(b) What is the special offer?   **1**

_____

* * * * *

13. What other information is given? Complete the sentences.   **2**

You have to _____.

For information, phone 06–82–02–25– _____.

* * * * *

Total (26)

[END OF QUESTION PAPER]

STANDARD GRADE | GENERAL
2012

OFFICIAL SQA PAST PAPERS 91 GENERAL FRENCH 2012

FOR OFFICIAL USE

G

Total

1000/29/01

NATIONAL THURSDAY, 10 MAY **FRENCH**
QUALIFICATIONS 10.50 AM – 11.35 AM **STANDARD GRADE**
2012 General Level
Reading

Fill in these boxes and read what is printed below.

Full name of centre: Linlithgow Academy

Town: Linlithgow

Forename(s): Kirstie Anne

Surname: Watson

Date of birth
Day 15 Month 08 Year 97 Scottish candidate number 063099856 Number of seat

When you are told to do so, open your paper and write your answers **in English** in the spaces provided.

You may use a French dictionary.

Before leaving the examination room you must give this book to the Invigilator. If you do not, you may lose all the marks for this paper.

SQA

PB 1000/29/01 6/27910

1. While you are on the Internet you read a profile which *Philippe Fournet* has prepared on www.fierdetreroutier.com, a website for lorry drivers.

> Bonjour! Mon nom est Philippe Fournet et je suis chauffeur routier depuis dix-sept ans. Normalement je transporte surtout des produits frais. Mais le problème, c'est que je dois souvent travailler la nuit pour livrer les produits sur les marchés très tôt le matin. J'aime bien ce métier parce que je voyage souvent à l'étranger et maintenant je suis responsable de la formation de nouveaux chauffeurs.

(a) For how long has Philippe been a long-distance lorry driver?

Seventeen years

(b) What does he normally transport?

Strawberries

(c) What problem does he often face? Mention any **one** thing.

I have to often work nights to deliver products to the market

(d) Why does Philippe really like this job? Mention any **one** thing.

I get holidays often.

2. An advert for an electric bike pops up.

> Aussi simple à utiliser qu'une bicyclette normale, le vélo électrique est équipé d'une batterie et d'un moteur qui vous aident à pédaler. Idéal pour les pistes cyclables et pour les pentes que vous montez sans vous fatiguer.

Tick (✓) **True** or **False** for each sentence.

	True	False
The electric bike is just as easy to use as an ordinary bike.	✓	
It is equipped with a battery instead of pedals.		✓
It is unsuitable for cycle tracks.		✓

[Turn over

3. You read an advert for a site offering free music downloads.

De la musique gratuite et légale sur Internet!

Vous pouvez écouter et télécharger des chansons originales. Les musiciens sont pleins de talent mais ne sont pas très connus. Si vous trouvez que leur musique est bonne, envoyez-leur un e-mail pour les encourager.

http://musique-légale.info/

Complete the sentences.

The musicians have a lot of talent but they are not _____well known_____.

If _____you like their music_____, send them an e-mail to encourage them.

4. You come across a forum for French teenagers where someone has posted the question "Should you do homework during the holidays?" Solène gives her opinion.

> Cette année, j'ai eu de mauvaises notes en maths parce que mon prof était affreux. Alors, il est nécessaire pour moi de faire des révisions pendant les vacances.
>
> Solène

Why will Solène be doing homework during the holidays? Mention any **one** thing.

She can do it as part of her revision

[Turn over

5. Cécile then gives her point of view.

> Moi, je suis pour les devoirs de vacances. Comme ça on est préparé pour la rentrée mais il faut les faire sans être forcé.
>
> Cécile

Why is Cécile in favour of holiday homework?

It will prepare you for your return

6. A boy called Kévin also gives his opinion on the forum.

> Moi, je dis "NON" aux devoirs pendant les vacances scolaires. Il faut profiter des vacances pour faire du sport, voyager, ou bien se reposer. A mon avis, tout le monde a besoin d'oublier les études pendant les vacances.
>
> Kévin

Apart from sport, what does Kévin say pupils should be doing during the holidays? Mention any **two** things.

To travel or put down all jollers

[Turn over

7. You then find an article about schools which do not close during the summer holidays.

Les vacances au collège

Pendant les grandes vacances, de nombreux collèges sont ouverts pour les élèves qui ne partent pas en vacances. Mais pas question de rester dans les classes! Par exemple, dans un collège à Saint-Denis, on organise beaucoup d'activités . . . on peut faire un stage avec les pompiers, visiter le château de Fontainebleau, enregistrer une chanson dans les studios de Radio Déclic ou même passer une journée dans un parc de loisirs!

(a) Why do some schools stay open during the summer holidays?

In case classes want to ask questions.

(b) What activities are offered at the school in Saint-Denis? Mention any **three** things.

visit the boat Fontainebleau, go to a radio station and go to the park for free time.

8. The article continues.

> Naturellement, le programme est très populaire. Les jeunes ont l'occasion d'apprendre de nouvelles choses en dehors du collège. Les jeunes disent qu'ils apprécient être avec leurs amis et rigoler au lieu de s'ennuyer à la maison.

(a) Why is the programme so popular? Mention **one** thing.

The popular activities

(b) Complete the sentence.

The young people say that they appreciate _the news thing_ and _outside the school_ instead of _being stuck inside_ at home.

[Turn over

9. You read another article with some ideas about how you can redecorate your bedroom on a limited budget.

CHACUN SON STYLE

Avec de l'imagination, il est possible de créer une déco sympa mais pas chère. Voici quelques conseils:

- Choisis ton style avant de changer ta décoration.
- Sélectionne deux ou trois couleurs pour changer les murs.
- Repeins de vieux meubles.
- Change l'ambiance en utilisant des ampoules de couleur.

Complete the sentences.

- Choose your style _to change the decorations_.
- Select _two to three colours to change_.
- Paint _any old furniture_.
- Change the atmosphere by _changing the colour_.

10. You then read about Yannick Noah, who is very popular in France and who has had two very different careers—tennis player and singer.

YANNICK NOAH

Yannick Noah est un personnage très célèbre en France. Comme joueur de tennis il a eu beaucoup de succès. A l'âge de 23 ans, il a gagné le grand tournoi français "Roland-Garros". En plus, comme capitaine, il a mené l'équipe de France de tennis à la victoire dans la Coupe Davis en 1991 et 1996. Sa carrière sportive terminée, Noah est devenu chanteur. Il a enregistré huit albums déjà et le septième, "Charango" s'est vendu à plus d' un million d'exemplaires!

(a) In what ways was Yannick successful in tennis? Mention any **two** things.

He had won the grand tournament of France "Roland-Garros" also and captained the "Coupe Davis" in 1991 and 1996

(b) What success has he had as a singer? Mention any **one** thing.

Sold 1 million copies

[Turn over for Question 11 on *Page twelve*

11. There is an interesting article giving advice to people learning to cook for themselves.

PREMIERS PLATS EN CUISINE

Tu ne sais pas cuisiner? Voici quelques conseils pour les chefs débutants.

- Vérifie que tu as tous les ingrédients nécessaires.
- Respecte les proportions exactes la première fois que tu essaies la recette.
- Laisse assez de temps pour cuire ton plat.
- Pour donner à la recette ta touche perso, ajoute un ingrédient que tu aimes.

Complete the sentences.

- Check that you have _the necessary ingredients_.
- Follow the exact proportions _for the recipe_.
- Leave enough time _to cook till its flat_.
- To give your recipe the personal touch _add 1 ingredient_.

Total (32)

[END OF QUESTION PAPER]

1000/29/12

NATIONAL QUALIFICATIONS 2012

THURSDAY, 10 MAY 11.55 AM – 12.20 PM (APPROX)

FRENCH
STANDARD GRADE
General Level
Listening Transcript

This paper must not be seen by any candidate.

The material overleaf is provided for use in an emergency only (eg the recording or equipment proving faulty) or where permission has been given in advance by SQA for the material to be read to candidates with additional support needs. The material must be read exactly as printed.

Transcript—General Level

> **Instructions to reader(s):**
>
> For each item, read the English **once**, then read the French **three times**, with an interval of 5 seconds between the readings. On completion of the third reading, pause for the length of time indicated in brackets after each item, to allow the candidates to write their answers.
>
> Where special arrangements have been agreed in advance to allow the reading of the material, those sections marked **(f)** should be read by a female speaker and those marked **(m)** by a male; those sections marked **(t)** should be read by the teacher.

(t) You are taking part in a school trip to France and you are staying in a youth hostel.

(m) or (f)   **Tu participes à une excursion scolaire en France et tu loges dans une auberge de jeunesse.**

(t) Question number one.

At the youth hostel you talk to a young French girl called Laure. She tells you about her journey the previous day. Complete the sentences.

(f)   **Hier nous avons fait le voyage en car. C'était très long et fatigant.**

(*30 seconds*)

(t) Question number two.

She tells you about the accommodation. What does she say? Mention any **one** thing.

(f)   **L'auberge a cinq étages et elle peut héberger cent personnes.**

(*30 seconds*)

(t) Question number three.

She tells you what facilities there are. What does she say? Complete the sentence.

(f)   **Il y a une piscine chauffée et un terrain de foot.**

(*30 seconds*)

(t) Question number four.

She tells you what she did last night. What does she say? Mention **two** things.

(f)   **Il y a beaucoup ici pour les jeunes. Hier soir j'ai joué au ping-pong et j'ai gagné! Après, on a mangé une glace pour célébrer ça.**

(*30 seconds*)

(t) Question number five.

Laure tells you about what she has planned for tomorrow. What does she say? Tick the **two** correct boxes.

(f)   **Demain on va visiter le marché dans le village. On doit prendre le petit déjeuner à huit heures quinze parce qu'on part à neuf heures et demie.**

(*30 seconds*)

(t) **Question number six.**

Laure tells you what the hostel has given her for a picnic. What does she have? Mention **three** things.

(f) **Regarde le pique-nique qu'on m'a donné pour aujourd'hui. J'ai un sandwich au jambon et des fromages de la région, et comme boisson, un jus de pomme.**

(*30 seconds*)

(t) **Question number seven.**

She tells you what the weather will be like tomorrow. What does she say? Mention any **two** things.

(f) **Demain on prévoit un temps variable—de la pluie le matin mais du soleil l'après-midi.**

(*30 seconds*)

(t) **Question number eight.**

You then talk to a boy called Philippe. He tells you about some of the rules in the youth hostel. What does he say? Mention **two** things.

(m) **Chaque soir on doit faire la vaisselle après le dîner et le matin il faut ranger la chambre.**

(*30 seconds*)

(t) **Question number nine.**

Philippe tells you what you are not allowed to do in the youth hostel after 10 pm. What does he say? Tick **three** boxes.

(m) **Tu sais, après dix heures du soir il est interdit d'entrer dans la cuisine, de faire du bruit ou de prendre une douche.**

(*30 seconds*)

(t) **Question number ten.**

Philippe tells you about one of the teachers, M. Dupont, who is supervising his group. What does he say? Mention any **three** things.

(m) **M. Dupont, c'est notre prof de chimie. Il est vraiment populaire parce qu'il donne des cours intéressants. En plus, il a un très bon sens de l'humour.**

(*30 seconds*)

(t) **Question number eleven.**

Philippe talks about his school. What does he say? Complete the sentence.

(m) **J'aime bien notre école parce que les salles de classe sont bien équipées et il y a des activités sportives après le collège.**

(*30 seconds*)

[*Turn over for Question 12 on Page four*

(t) Question number twelve.

He talks about going back to school after the holidays. What does he say? Complete the sentences.

(m) **Alors, après les grandes vacances je serai en troisième. Je devrai faire deux heures de devoirs chaque soir donc il sera difficile de sortir avec mes copains pendant la semaine.**

(30 seconds)

(t) End of test.
Now look over your answers.

[END OF TRANSCRIPT]

FOR OFFICIAL USE

Total Mark

1000/29/02

NATIONAL QUALIFICATIONS 2012

THURSDAY, 10 MAY 11.55 AM – 12.20 PM (APPROX)

FRENCH STANDARD GRADE
General Level
Listening

Fill in these boxes and read what is printed below.

Full name of centre

Linlithgow Academy

Town

Linlithgow

Forename(s)

Kirstie Anne

Surname

Watson

Date of birth

Day	Month	Year	Scottish candidate number	Number of seat
15	08	97	063099856	

When you are told to do so, open your paper.

You will hear a number of short items in French. You will hear each item three times, then you will have time to write your answer.

Write your answers, **in English**, in this book, in the appropriate spaces.

You may take notes as you are listening to the French, but only in this book.

You may **not** use a French dictionary.

You are not allowed to leave the examination room until the end of the test.

Before leaving the examination room you must give this book to the Invigilator. If you do not, you may lose all the marks for this paper.

You are taking part in a school trip to France and you are staying in a youth hostel.

Tu participes à une excursion scolaire en France et tu loges dans une auberge de jeunesse.

1. At the youth hostel you talk to a young French girl called Laure. She tells you about her journey the previous day. Complete the sentences.

   Yesterday we travelled _____ .

   It was very long and _____ .

   * * * * *

2. She tells you about the accommodation. What does she say? Mention any **one** thing.

   _____

   * * * * *

3. She tells you what facilities there are. What does she say? Complete the sentence.

   There's a _____ swimming pool and a

   _____ .

   * * * * *

4. She tells you what she did last night. What does she say? Mention **two** things.

   _____

   _____

   * * * * *

Marks

5. Laure tells you about what she has planned for tomorrow. What does she say? Tick (✓) the **two** correct boxes.

2

She is going to visit the church in the village.	
She is going to visit the market in the village.	
She is going to have breakfast at 8.15.	
She is going to have breakfast at 9.30.	

* * * * *

6. Laure tells you what the hostel has given her for a picnic. What does she have? Mention **three** things.

3

_____

_____

_____

* * * * *

7. She tells you what the weather will be like tomorrow. What does she say? Mention any **two** things.

2

_____

_____

* * * * *

[*Turn over*

Marks

8. You then talk to a boy called Philippe. He tells you about some of the rules in the youth hostel. What does he say? Mention **two** things.

2

_____

_____

* * * * *

9. Philippe tells you what you are not allowed to do in the youth hostel after 10 pm. What does he say? Tick (✓) **three** boxes.

3

You are not allowed to . . .

. . . visit someone else's room.	
. . . play music.	
. . . go into the kitchen.	
. . . use the games room.	
. . . make a noise.	
. . . have a shower.	

* * * * *

10. Philippe tells you about one of the teachers, M. Dupont, who is supervising his group. What does he say? Mention any **three** things.

3

_____

_____

_____

* * * * *

Marks

11. Philippe talks about his school. What does he say? Complete the sentence.   2

I like our school because the classrooms are _____

and there are _____ after school.

* * * * *

12. He talks about going back to school after the holidays. What does he say? Complete the sentences.   2

After the summer holidays, I will be in fourth year. I will have to do

_____ each evening, so it will be difficult

to _____ during the week.

* * * * *

Total (26)

[END OF QUESTION PAPER]

Acknowledgements

Permission has been sought from all relevant copyright holders and Bright Red Publishing is grateful for the use of the following:

An image of an ipod © Apple Computer Ltd (2009 Reading page 6);
An extract and photo taken from www.fierdetreroutier.com © Philippe Fournet (2012 Reading page 2).

STANDARD GRADE | ANSWER SECTION

BrightRED ANSWER SECTION FOR
SQA STANDARD GRADE GENERAL FRENCH 2008–2012

FRENCH GENERAL READING 2008

1. (a) Full/complete/three course meal/ lunch/dinner/evening meal
   or
   Starter/entree/first course/main course/meal and dessert/sweet/pudding

   (b) To win tickets/(get) free tickets/win a (free) meal/get a free meal/give out/away tickets/ complimentary tickets

2. • Put their health/their health is
   • <u>Less than</u> 5€
   • Heart problems/disease
   • <u>Fresh</u> produce/products/food(s)

3. (a) (A label with your) name, address and telephone number
   or
   A label/tag/card/ticket with your/personal details/information/ID/any two specifics/a label with contact details

   (b) When/if the label has come off (the outside of the bag)
   NB If the word "label" is mentioned in (a), there must be an indication in (b) that this is a different label.

4. (a) *Any two from:*
   • To/you get/choose the best offer(s)
   • Book/reserve a last-minute flight/make reservation at the last minute/book (a flight/seat/ticket) at the last minute/a late flight/last-minute deals
   • To plan/prepare a business/leisure trip/ holiday

   (b) *Any two from:*
   • Timetables/flight times/the times planes will be leaving
   • Car hire/rental
   • (Car-) parking <u>costs/charges/tariffs</u>/price of car parks/car park costs

5. • Marcel (Bordeaux)
   • Adrienne (Paris)
   • Georges (Marseille)

6. • False
   • True
   • False
   • True

7. • How many hours <u>per day</u>
   • Tidy their room
   • Wash/do/clean the dishes/do the washing up
   • <u>Listening</u> to music
   • Going/being <u>out with friends</u>

8. (a) Cheaper <u>train/rail</u> fares/reductions/get money off/discounts on <u>trains</u>

   (b) *Any one from:*
   • Electric(al)/electronic (goods/appliances) <u>shop(s)</u>/shop(s) which sell electrical/household goods/appliances
   • <u>Public/municipal/council/local/town</u> (swimming) pool(s)/baths

   (c) *Any one from:*
   • Driving schools
   • Insurance companies
   • Car/motor dealerships/showrooms/ salesmen/sellers/dealers

9. (a) An English test/exam/test on her English speaking/pass a test/exam in English

   (b) *Any two from:*
   • Gives out/serves/distributes/delivers meals/food
   • Serves drinks
   • Makes (sure)/the/her passengers (are) comfortable

   (c) • Reassure passengers/keep passengers calm/keep passengers from worrying/tell the passengers not to worry
   • Help them (get) out of/exit/leave/evacuate the plane/get them out of the plane/show them out of the plane

FRENCH GENERAL LISTENING 2008

1. (a) On the second floor
   (b) (From/at) 7·30 (am)

2. • (On/to the) right of reception
   • Free

3. 15 minutes <u>by car</u>/a fifteen minute <u>drive</u>

4. (a) In the country(side)
   (b) (To be at/next to/by/beside/near) the sea(side)/ beach/coast because the sea(side)/beach/coast is great/super

5. • Is this your first visit to this area?
   • How long are you staying here?

6. *Any two from:*
   • Get a tan/sunbathe/lie in the sun (at/on the beach)
   • Go <u>wind</u>-surfing (at the beach)
   • Go horse-riding

7. • His sister is happy to be on holiday
   • At Easter she worked hard for her exams
   • She wants to go to university in October

8. (a) *Any one from:*
      • He has/owns a (an electrical) shop/He is a shopkeeper/shop proprietor
      • He <u>sells</u> electrical items/goods/products/appliances/<u>sells</u> fridges/<u>sells</u> washing machines
   (b) In the Tourist Office/Tourist Information Centre/Tourist Board

9. *Any two from:*
   • There's lots for <u>young people/children/kids/teenagers/youths/youngsters</u> to do
   • She can spend time with/be with her husband/his mum and dad can spend time together
   • <u>The/her children</u> are always busy/doing things/doing activities
   or
   <u>The/her children</u> are with their friends/other young people

10. (a) *Any one from:*
       • Hire/rent bikes/a bike
       • (Go) cycling/(go for) a cycle run/tour (round/to the town)
    (b) <u>Outside/in front of</u> the hotel <u>after</u> lunch/dinner/the meal/they have eaten

11. • False
    • False
    • True

12. • Computing/IT/ICT/computer technology/ information systems/computer systems/computer science/information studies
    • In Germany
    • (New/computer) software/<u>computer</u> program(s)

FRENCH GENERAL READING 2009

1. • 3000 children/pupils
   • Money/financial problems/issues
   • 130€ <u>per/a month</u>

2. (a) *Any two from:*
      • Presenting/reading/reporting <u>the news on TV</u>
      • Doing a report/reporting in/from the USA/America/going to the USA to do a report
      • Covering/reporting on a sports <u>event/meeting/tournament/match/competition</u>
   (b) *Any two from:*
      • Curiosity/inquisitiveness/should be curious/inquisitive/nosey
      • <u>Know how to/be able to/can</u> express/put across (his) ideas
      • Get on (well) with/connect with/have good relations(hips) with people/be good with people/be a people person

3. • Youngest
   • Alone/solo/single-handed/(by) himself/on his own
   • (From) a <u>few/some/several/a couple of/only</u> kilometres away/back/behind/a distance of a <u>few/some</u> kilometres
   • Do/finish/catch up with (his/some) homework/schoolwork/studies

4.

T	F
✓	
	✓
✓	
	✓
	✓

5. (a) • Rich/well off/wealthy (people)/people with (lots of) money
       • People who are afraid of downloading
   (b) *Any one from:*
       • (They risk) losing/(might/will) lose (lots of) money/they don't/won't make/get money
       • Some people download from an illegal site/download illegally
   (c) There will be advertising/an advert/a pop-up

6. (a) *Any two from:*
      • Fingerprints
      • Handprints
      • Voice (recognition/identification)
      • Eye(s) (recognition/identification)
   (b) • (Bank/credit) cards will/would/may/might not be necessary/essential
   (c) *Any one from:*
      • You will place your hand on a screen/with a hand scan
      • You will put your eye in front of a camera/you will look into a camera/with an eye scan

7. (a) • His (good) friend is annoying/irritating/tiresome/ being a nuisance/a pain/gets on his nerves
         or
         His friend copies/ imitates him
   (b) *Any one from:*
      • He laughs when Marc laughs
      • Copies/uses/speaks in his accent/voice (when telling jokes)

8. • His friend/he lacks confidence/needs (more) confidence/has problems with confidence/has low/no confidence
   • Encourage/help/persuade him to show his (own/proper/real/true) personality/be himself
   or
   Encourage/help/persuade him to have his own/proper/real/true personality

9. • Throw/put/dump electronic/electric(al) equipment/electronics in the bin/bucket
   • (Very) few/not many
   • Tyre(s)
   • Toys

FRENCH GENERAL LISTENING 2009

1. *Any one from:*
   • Magnificent/great (weather)
   • 25 degrees/25°

2. • Hundred
   • Box(es)/tin(s) of chocolate(s)

3. (a) • Near/close to the station
   (b) • Three cars/vehicles crashed/collided

4. (a) • A mobile (phone)
   (b) • What is the name of/who is/name the President of France/what is the President of France's name?

5. • Did you enjoy your trip/ have a good/nice/pleasant journey/trip/how was your journey?

6. • Eat in the/your (bed)room(s)/take food to/have food in your room
   • (Have a/use the) shower

7. • A (small) games room/area
   • (a) tennis (court/courts)

8. • (Several/lots of) historical sites/places/landmarks/monuments/buildings/ attractions (to visit/see/go to)
   • (You can go to the) theme park(s)

9. • Have you visited France before?
   • How long will you be staying here?

10. *Any one from:*
    • It's in the north-west
    • It's (very) old

11. **History**
    • Favourite/preferred subject
    • Teacher is young

    Maths
    • Hates/doesn't like it/maths is horrible
    • (Lessons are) boring

12. • False
    • True
    • False

13. • Her group/she is going on a tour of/in the town/city/going to tour (round) the town/city/going into town for/on a tour/going to visit/ see the town /go sightseeing in the town
    • They are leaving/going in fifteen minutes.

FRENCH GENERAL READING 2010

1. (a) • She was a hardworking pupil
      • She dreamed of the cinema

   (b) *Any two from:*
       • (You have to) have confidence/be confident
       • (You have to) work (hard/well)/do your best at school
       • It's not (an) easy (profession/job)/don't think it's easy
       • There are lots of people who would like/want to be famous

   (c) • Parent(s)/they/the family didn't have (enough/the/much/any/a lot of) money/couldn't afford them/it

2. (a) *Any one from:*
       • Don't panic/keep/stay calm
       • Ask/talk/speak to/get help from your/the/a teacher
       • Look (for explanations) in/at your book(s)

   (b) *Any two from:*
       • Say/repeat them out loud/aloud
       • Write them (out/down) several/many/lots of times/write them (out/down) repeatedly
       • Ask/get your friend(s) to ask you/pose questions/test/quiz you

3. *Any two from:*
   • (Get/have a minimum of/at least) 8 hours sleep
   • Eat/have a balanced/good diet/eat/have (a) balanced meal(s)/eat well/healthily/good food/take (the/your) time to eat well/healthily/good food
     or
     Forget the/don't diet
   • Do/practise/take part in (physical) exercise/(a/one) physical activity every/per/a day/exercise every day

4. • Get up/have to/must be up (very) early
   • Help my father
   • Being outdoors/outside/out
   • (Always/very) hungry/starving/famished

5. • He goes out with his friends
   • He buys fashionable clothes

6. (a) • 8 day/one week course/training

   (b) *Any one from:*
       • You/we/they get/will have/be accompanied by a(n) (experienced) guide
       • You will stay in a youth hostel

   (c) • Equipment/gear/kit is provided

7. *Any two from:*
   • Accommodation is high in the mountains
   • Magnificent view(s)
   • Lots of sporting activities
     or
     sporting activities for young people
   • Ideal/perfect for (people who like) active/action/activity holidays
     or
     Ideal/perfect for (people who like)/outdoor holidays/holidays in the open/fresh air

8. *Any three from:*
   • 3 nights, breakfast included/3 nights B&B
   • (Unlimited travel on) public transport
   • (Free) entry into museums
   • Cruise/boat trip on the Seine/river

9. • At the hottest/hotter/warmest/warmer time(s)/hour(s)
   • (about/around/roughly/approximately) 1.5 l(itres) of water per day
   • an air-conditioned place/area/room

10. • Cut/kept it short/had short hair
    • Hide/cover (up)/mask/get rid of the smell(s)/odour(s) Make them smell better
    • Take regular baths/bath(e) regularly
    • Have a shower/showers/are equipped/fitted with a shower
    • Don't use/brush their teeth with

FRENCH GENERAL LISTENING 2010

1. • <u>Your</u> reservation/confirmation
   or
   Letter/proof/details of reservation/letter of confirmation
   • Identification/(proof of) ID

2. • 7.00
   • 9.30
   • Self-service/buffet/help yourself

3. • 3rd floor/floor 3
   • Opposite/facing/in front of the lift/elevator

4. • When did you arrive?
   • How long are you staying here?

5. • True
   • False
   • True

6. *Any two from:*
   • Doesn't (really) like it
   • Lots of/too many cars/vehicles/too much/a lot of traffic (in the streets/on the roads)
   • It's (very) polluted

7. *Any two from:*
   • Sunbathing/getting a tan/tanning
   • <u>Long</u> walks
   or
   Walks <u>on the beach</u>
   • Water-sports

8. • She is a student/at university
   • She is going/training/wants to be a <u>History</u> teacher

9. • With the school/a school group/my class/on a school trip
   • Edinburgh castle
   • The (beautiful) mountains

10. (*a*) • Wednesday morning
    (*b*) • In the (town) square
    or
    In front of/outside the town hall

11. • Sunglasses
    • (Bottle of) wine

12. • It's free

FRENCH GENERAL READING 2011

1. • (Hill)walking/walks/hikes/hiking (up the mountains)/rambling
   • Not (very/too) far (away)/(quite/fairly) close/near(by)

2. • Its own/a different language/tongue/a language called/people who speak Breton
   • Traditional music festivals

3. (*a*) • He talks/chats/they (all) talk/chat <u>about everything/all sorts of things</u>
   • He has/they have fun/a laugh/he laughs/jokes/they laugh/joke
   (*b*) • When he is (working) on the computer/laptop
   • When he is reading (in his bedroom)

4. • Chair<u>s</u>/seat<u>s</u> against/along/(a)round/at/ beside the wall(s)
   • Plastic dishes/crockery/plate<u>s</u>
   • Stay/remain/keep/be in touch/contact/be contactable (in case there is/are any problem(s)/trouble)
   • Tell/inform the neighbour(s) (about the party)
   • No-one dances/people won't/don't (like to) dance/don't want to dance

5. (*a*) *Any one from:*
   • Factories/factory
   • (In the) Army
   (*b*) *Any one from:*
   • Repetitive
   • Dangerous
   • Hard/difficult
   (*c*) *Any one from:*
   • Cooking/making meals/food
   • Housework/chores/household tasks/work
   (*d*) • Vacuum cleaners (which clean on their own)

6. • Four hours <u>per/a/every/each day</u>

7. • Obese/<u>too</u> fat/<u>too</u> large/<u>too</u> big/<u>too</u> overweight
   • Eat <u>lots of /many</u> sweet/sugary things/foods/sweets
   • Exercise <u>enough</u>

8. • Does not/won't go to school/goes to school
   • Get married/have children (very/too) <u>early/young</u>
   • Finish/complete their studies/schooling/education/school

9. (*a*) *Any one from:*
   • Restaurant menu(s)
   • Room service (menu(s)/food)
   (*b*) • He (has to) <u>create(s)/make(s</u> up)/<u>do(es)</u> (a) special menu(s)
   (*c*) • Prepare/make/create/try (a) <u>new</u> dish(es)/recipe(s)/course(s)/something <u>new</u>
   (*d*) *Any one from:*
   • He tastes/tries/samples them/it (personally)
   • <u>If he likes them/it</u> he adds them/it to/puts them/it on the menu
   (*e*) *Any one from:*
   • (It's a job where) you/he work(s) hard/it's hard (work)
   • (It's a job with/he has) no fixed/set hours
   • It's (also) his passion/he loves it

10. (a) *Any one from:*
    - They are important days/dates in (their) history/they are important historical days/dates
    - You don't (have to) go to school/no school
    - You don't (have to) go to work/no work

    (b) • For an 8 hour (working) day

    (c) • Soldiers who died for France

FRENCH GENERAL LISTENING 2011

1. • Not for him/me/not his/my thing

2. *Any one from:*
   - Uniform/it costs a lot/is expensive/dear
   - It's difficult for big/large families

3. • The school is old (box 1)
   • Her English teacher is nice (box 4)

4. • Young people/youth(s)/children/kids/teenagers/the young
   • Open-air/outdoor/outside

5. *Any two from:*
   - He walks his/the dog/puppy/takes his/the dog/puppy out
   - Chats/talks/speaks with his friend(s)
   - Watches/goes to (see) (a) football (match)/ goes to a/the (football) match/the football (at the stadium)

6. *Any two from:*
   - Wash/clean the car
   - Set/lay the table (every evening/day)
   - Tidy her bedroom/keep her room tidy

7. • True
   • False
   • False

8. • The bus/bus fares/journeys (for going into the town/city)
   • (Buying) clothes

9. (a) (A) ticket(s) for a concert (tonight)

   (b) What is the capital of Spain?

10. • The (train/railway) station
    • Right
    • Third (street/road/turning/opening)

11. *Any two from:*
    - Magnificent (day)
    - A few/some clouds/a bit cloudy
    - 29 degrees

12. (a) • (Next/this) Saturday

    (b) • A group of four pays for three (people/meals)/four for three

13. • Book/reserve (in advance)
    • 85

FRENCH GENERAL READING 2012

1. (a) • 17 years
   (b) • Fresh produce/products/food(s)
   (c) *Any one from:*
   • Has to work at night/during the night/nights
   • Has to deliver (produce to the markets) <u>early in the morning</u>/needs to be at the market(s) <u>early in the morning</u>/the market(s) want the produce <u>early in the morning</u>
   (d) *Any one from:*
   • Travelling <u>abroad</u>/visiting (other/different) countries/<u>foreign</u> places
   • Training/teaching/instructing (new) drivers

2. • True
   • False
   • False

3. • (Very) well-known/famous
   • If (you think) their/the music is good/if you like/enjoy/rate their/the music

4. *Any one from:*
   • She got bad/poor marks/grades/results <u>in maths</u>
   • Her <u>maths</u> teacher was terrible/awful/dreadful/bad
   • <u>She needs to/must/has to</u> revise/<u>it is necessary for her</u> to revise

5. • (So that) you/we are/she is prepared/ready for going back to/returning to school/classes/work/(the start of) the new (school) year/term

6. • *Any two from:*
   Travelling/going on holiday/vacation/on a journey/a trip/away
   • Resting/relaxing
   • Forgetting/not thinking about studies/studying/school work

7. (a) • For the pupils/children/people who don't/can't go on holiday/stay at home
   (b) *Any three from:*
   • Train/do training/a (training) course/work experience with firemen/the fire brigade/as a fireman
   • Visit a/the castle (of Fontainebleau)
   • Record a song/songs
   • Go to a theme/leisure park

8. (a) • Young people/pupils/they/you (have the opportunity/occasion to) learn/do <u>new</u> things (outwith/outside school)
   (b) • <u>Being/meeting/hanging about/getting together with</u> (their) friend<u>s</u>
   • Laughing/joking/having fun/a laugh/a joke/a carry on/a good time
   • (Getting/being) bored

9. • <u>Before</u> changing the decor/decoration/the interior design/(re)decorating/you (begin to) decorate
   • 2 or 3 colours to change/paint the wall<u>s</u>/ for the wall<u>s</u>
   • Old (piece<u>s</u> of) furniture
   • Using (a) coloured (light) bulb(s)

10. (a) *Any two from:*
    • (At 23) he won the biggest/a big/major French tournament/Roland Garros/the French Open
    • He was captain of the French/Davis Cup team (in 1991 and 1996)
    • He/they/the French team won the Davis Cup (in 1991 and 1996)
    (b) *Any one from:*
    • He has recorded/made/released 8 albums
    • His 7th album/one of his albums/Charango (has) sold (more than) 1/a million

11. • <u>All</u> the (necessary) ingredients/(all) the <u>necessary/required/right</u> ingredients/the ingredients <u>you need/require</u>
    • The first time (you try/make the/a recipe)
    • To cook your dish/food/it/to let it cook
    • Add an ingredient you like/love

FRENCH GENERAL LISTENING 2012

1. - By coach/bus
   - Tiring/exhausting

2. *Any one from:*
   - Has five floors/storeys/levels
   - Can take/sleep/accommodate/hold 100 (people)/its capacity is 100 (people)

3. - Heated
   - Football pitch/ground/park/field/area

4. - She played/won at table tennis/ping-pong
   - She had/ate an ice cream (to celebrate)
     or
     She celebrated (by having an ice cream)

5. - She's going to visit the market in the village
   - She's going to have breakfast at 8.15

6. - Ham sandwich(es)
   - Regional/local cheese(s)/cheese(s) from the area
   - Apple juice

7. *Any two from:*
   - Changeable/variable/varied/mixed
   - Rain in the morning
   - Sunny/sun in the afternoon/after midday/lunch

8. - (Have to) do the washing up/wash/clean the dishes
   - Tidy the (bed)room(s)

9. - Go into the kitchen
   - Make a noise
   - Have a shower

10. *Any three from:*
    - Chemistry teacher
    - (Really/very) popular
    - Interesting lesson(s)/class(es)
    - (Good) sense of humour

11. - Well equipped
    - Sporting activities/sports activities/clubs

12. - 2 hours homework/study(ing)/studies
    - Go out with my friends

Hey! I've done it

BrightRED
PUBLISHING

© 2012 SQA/Bright Red Publishing Ltd, All Rights Reserved
Published by Bright Red Publishing Ltd, 6 Stafford Street, Edinburgh, EH3 7AU
Tel: 0131 220 5804, Fax: 0131 220 6710, enquiries: sales@brightredpublishing.co.uk,
www.brightredpublishing.co.uk

Official SQA answers to 978-1-84948-245-5
2008-2012